ThiNking Hats

Book 2

Mrs T. Jones

Anna Forsyth

Mrs T. Jones

Curriculum Concepts

comprehensive coverage

C000179708

Thinking Hats

ISBN 9781906125578

Ordering Code – UK0151

Curriculum Concepts UK

The Old School

Upper High Street

Bedlinog

Mid-Glamorgan CF46 6SA

Email: orders@curriculumconcepts.co.uk

www.curriculumconcepts.co.uk

Contents

Introduction

Why Thinking Hats?

Have you ever heard the phrase, "Put your thinking caps on."? We often use it when faced with a situation that requires focused thinking. Whether it is a complex problem or a simple decision, there are many occasions when purposeful thinking is required. In an age of easy access to new information and technology, it is important to teach students not what to think, but *how* to think. In his book *Six Thinking Hats*, Edward De Bono* has created a six-hat system that trains students to focus their thinking for specific purposes, and to think in new ways, such as weighing up positive and negative outcomes and looking at the bigger picture. Each hat is a different colour, and represents a different way of thinking. This book is a collection of lessons that you can use in your classroom using the thinking hats concept. At the back of this book you will find a reference chart that explains the hats in more detail.

* De Bono, E. *Six Thinking Hats.*

Boston, Mass., U.S.A. Little, Brown and Company, (1st Back Pay paperback edition, rev. and updated.) 1999.

How to Use This Book

This book is divided into curriculum areas; Art, Music, PHSE and Citizenship, Physical Education, Geography, History, English, Design and Technology, Mathematics and Science. For most curriculum areas there are two easy-to-use lesson plans at two levels of difficulty – Year 2/3 and Year 3/4. Some lesson plans have more than one related curriculum area.

The lessons are suggestions only, and can be adapted to meet the needs of your students.

At the back of the book are templates (pages 41-47) that are required for the lessons;
- The Colour Wheel
  - cards with a picture of a hat with the colour and a graphic to assist with recognition,
  - cards for each hat with key questions to ask (to be photocopied onto the back of the hats)
- A Thinking Hats Reference Chart which summarises what each hat represents.
- A Hat template.
- Thinking Hats key words on cards to be photocopied.

As you become more confident with using the 'Thinking Hats' concept all these templates can be incorporated into everyday activities. The more your students use the thinking hats concept the better their thinking skills will become.

When introducing the hats, it is best to teach them as a separate unit before incorporating them in to other areas. For younger children, consider introducing each hat separately so they understand what each hat means/represents and what they have to think about. Before you begin, take the time to read the Thinking Hats Reference Chart at the back of this book and familiarise yourself with the six hats.

Teachers will need to give some forethought into the amount of supervision, guidance and teacher participation given to help students work through the activities in the series. Students' ages and abilities will play a factor in these and the degree to which students are to work independently. Happy thinking!

Hat Dance

Teacher's Notes

Group/Class Size: Group of 4 or 5
Duration: 20-30 minutes

Lesson Objective(s):

• Students will initiate and express dance ideas based on a variety of stimuli.

Learning outcomes:

• Students will use thinking hats as stimuli to create their own dance ideas, using the theme of people who wear hats.

Write your own learning outcome(s) here:

Point(s) to Ponder:

You may want to start a props or costume box of different hats for your classroom.

You will need:

• Thinking hats cards or wheel
• An assortment of hats
• Music of your choice

Activity

★ Split into groups of four or five.

★ Pick a thinking hats card or spin the wheel.

★ Make up a dance as a group. The theme for your dance is: "People who wear hats".

★ You could use the thinking hats as follows:

Black hat: Someone who wears a hat that makes them appear negative, or something negative that could happen if you wear a hat.

Yellow hat: Someone who wears a hat with a positive effect, or something great that could happen if you wear a hat

Red hat: How someone might feel or react to something when they wear a particular hat.

Green hat: What unique or unusual people wear hats? What is something you wouldn't normally do while wearing that hat? Be creative.

Blue hat: Use one hat as a starting point for your whole dance.

Cultural Dance

Teacher's Notes

Group/Class Size: Any
Duration: 20-30 minutes (Over several lessons)

Lesson Objective(s):
* Students will demonstrate an awareness of dance as part of community life.

Learning outcomes:
* Students will learn a cultural dance.
* Students will use thinking hats to discuss dance in a particular culture and/or community and make a wall display.

Write your own learning outcome(s) here:

Point(s) to Ponder:
* This lesson could complement studying a particular culture.
* If you have an expert from a particular nationality in your class, this would be a great opportunity for them to share their culture with the class.
* Why not make a day of it and have a special meal as well!

You will need:
* Thinking hats cards or wheel
* An expert who can teach a cultural dance
* Paper and art materials to make a display

* ★ Bring in people who can talk to you about what dance means to them in their culture or community.
* ★ Use the thinking hats to come up with questions to ask them, and make up a display of what you find out.

White hat: What are some facts about dance in that culture? What do you wear? Is there anything special that you have to do? When do you perform this dance?

Yellow hat: What do they enjoy about dancing in their culture? What are the good things about it?

Red hat: Emotions or feelings. Do you like to dance? Why? Do you have any special memories about dance?

Black hat: What do you want to change about the dance? What don't you like?

Green hat: What is new or unique about dance in this culture?

* ★ Have one of these people teach you one of their dances.
* ★ Learn a cultural dance, which you can perform at assembly or for friends and family.

Red Alert

Teacher's Notes

Group/Class Size: Any/groups of 4 or 5
Duration: 30-45 minutes (2-3 lessons)

Lesson Objective(s):
- Students will explore through movement, combine and contrast the dance elements of body awareness, space, time, energy and relationships.

Learning outcomes:
- Students will use the red thinking hat to explore through movement the elements of body awareness, space and time.
- Students will create a dance sequence around the theme of emotions, using body awareness, space and time.

Write your own learning outcome(s) here:

Point(s) to ponder:
- You may like to explore how different music works with different emotions.

You will need:

- Red thinking hat
- Contrasting music

Activity

★ Discuss the red thinking hat and what it stands for.

★ Split into groups of four to five students.

★ In your groups:
Brainstorm how you could use body awareness, space and time to show different emotions.

★ Choose two contrasting emotions and make a short, two-part dance sequence to show to the rest of the class.

★ See if the class can guess which emotions were being displayed.

★ Which elements or movements are good for showing certain emotions?

★ Build a collection or list of movements that show emotions to use in future dances.

Traffic Lights

Teacher's Notes

Group/Class Size: Any
Duration: 30-45 minutes

Lesson Objective(s):
*   Students will select, combine, and use elements of dance to develop ideas.

Learning outcomes:
*   Students will use the green, red and yellow hats to select and use dance elements in a dance sequence.

Write your own learning outcome(s) here:

Point(s) to Ponder:
*   Consider having prizes or awards/certificates for the most creative movements, best use of elements, most emotive dance etc.

You will need:

*   Green, yellow and red thinking hat cards
*   A cardboard traffic light or signal (make the amber light yellow)
*   Contrasting music

Activity

★ Set up a traffic light or three circles painted green, red and yellow.

★ Nominate one person to be the traffic warden.

★ Turn the music on. Dance freestyle, using elements of dance such as space, time and body awareness (nominated by the teacher).

★ When the music stops, traffic warden holds up one of the thinking hats colours. For example:

Green hat: Be as creative as possible.

Red hat: Choose an emotion that you want to show through your movements.

Yellow hat: Dance freestyle using dance elements, but you must keep a smile on your face at all times or you are out. (Look around at all those cheesy grins!)

★ Swap around and take turns being the traffic warden.

★ Keep going until you feel you have been able to express each of the hats well.

Once Again, with Feeling!

Teacher's Notes

Group/Class Size: In pairs
Duration: 30-45 minutes

Lesson Objective(s):
* Students will contribute and develop ideas in drama based on personal experience, imagination, and other stimuli.

Learning outcomes:
* Students will use the red thinking hat to develop ideas in a short drama sequence, showing different emotions.

Write your own learning outcome(s) here:

You will need:
* Red thinking hat card
* Props or costumes if desired
* A buzzer or musical instrument

Activity

* ★ As a class, choose a problem, situation or event and make up a short drama in pairs based on a conversation between two people.

* ★ Use the red hat to think of different emotions that could be involved in the drama.

* ★ Use the questions on the red thinking hat card to explore the emotions of the characters.

* ★ When the buzzer sounds or the instrument is played, re-play the scene using a different emotion.

* ★ Repeat as many times as you like.

* ★ Show your drama to the rest of the class.

Drama Class

Subject: English: Drama

Teacher's Notes

Year: 2/3

Group/Class Size: Any
Duration: 30-45 minutes (3-4 lessons)

Lesson Objective(s):

*   Students will identify drama as a part of everyday life and recognised that it serves a variety of purposes.

Learning outcomes:

*   Students will use the thinking hats to interview a special drama guest to find out more about drama and its purposes.
*   Students will make a short dramatised interview and video.

Write your own learning outcome(s) here:

Point(s) to Ponder:

*   To include everyone, you may like to add roles such as cameraperson, producer, make-up and hair people, and audience.

You will need:

*   Thinking hats cards or wheel
*   A special guest who is involved in drama eg. an actor, playwright, cameraperson or drama teacher
*   A video camera (optional)

★ As a class, spend time using the thinking hats to form questions that you want to ask your guest. For example:

White hat: Facts. What do you have to do in your job? Is it hard? What are some examples of your work?

Yellow hat: What do you like about your job/drama?

Black hat: What do you not like about your job/drama? Are there any negative aspects to your work?

Red hat: How do you show emotions? Have you had any experiences in working in drama when you felt emotional?

Blue hat: Why did you get into drama? What does drama mean for you?

Green hat: What was the strangest experience you have had? What are the creative parts of your job?

★ After your interview, use the information to re-make a short drama of an

Analyze This!

Teacher's Notes

Group/Class Size: Any
Duration: 30-45 minutes (2 lessons)

Lesson Objective(s):

* Students will present and respond to drama, identifying ways in which elements of drama combine with ideas to create meaning.

Learning outcomes:

* Students will view a play, video or short drama sequence and respond, using thinking hats to discuss and identify elements of drama and how meaning was created.

Write your own learning outcome(s) here:

Point(s) to Ponder:

* This could be a field trip to see a play or performance as a class.

You will need:

* Thinking hats cards or wheel
* A short drama sequence, play, video or performance

Activity

★ As a class, view a play or performance and using thinking hats, analyze the drama elements and how meaning was developed.

Yellow hat: What was good about the way the drama developed?

Blue hat: Did you understand the meaning of the drama as a whole? What were the main ideas?

White hat: What elements of drama were used in the play? How did they show the meaning of the drama or play?

Green hat: Could you think of any way you could have done the play better? (Think creatively.)

Black hat: What didn't work so well in the play? What did you dislike?

Red hat: How did the play make you feel? What emotions did the characters go through?

★ Make a class presentation of, or brainstorm what you learned.

Special Guest

Teacher's Notes

Group/Class Size: Any
Duration: 30-45 minutes

Lesson Objective(s):

• Students will initiate and develop ideas with others and improvise drama in a range of situations.

Learning outcomes:

• Students will use thinking hats as a basis for improvising in drama.

Write your own learning outcome(s) here:

You will need:

• Thinking hats cards or wheel
• Props or costumes if desired
• A good dose of imagination

Activity

This game is called Guess Who:

★ Choose one person to act as the host of a party.

★ Three other people are guests at this party who arrive one at a time.

★ Before they arrive at the party, the guests are given a thinking hat card. During the drama they are to introduce themselves and then answer questions from the host, but they are only allowed to talk in the following way:

Red hat: Feelings and emotions

White hat: Facts and figures

Green hat: Off the topic/random/weird/make the conversation take a different turn.

Yellow hat: Positive comments only

Black hat: Negative comments only

★ The job of the people in the audience is to guess which hat the guests are wearing.

★ Take turns at being a guest and being in the audience.

One music, many uses

Subject: Music

Year: 2/3

Teacher's Notes

Group/Class Size: In groups
Duration: 30-45 minutes

Lesson Objective(s):

* Students will identify music as part of everyday life and recognised that it serves a variety of purposes.

Learning outcomes:

* Students will use thinking hats to discuss the different purposes and uses of music.
* Students will make a chart about the different purposes and uses of music.

Write your own learning outcome(s) here:

You will need:

* Thinking hats cards or wheel
* Large piece of paper and pens
* Art supplies

Activity

★ In groups, discuss the different purposes and uses of music using the thinking hats as a guide.

Red hat: How can you use music to change your emotions?

Yellow hat: What positive things can music be used for?

Black hat: What negative ways can you use music?

Green hat: What crazy/weird/creative uses or purposes can you think of for music?

White hat: List all the purposes for music that you can think of.

Blue hat: Are there any patterns or themes that you can see?

★ Make a wall chart to display what you learned.

★ Use your green hat to make it creative.

Compare & Contrast

Teacher's Notes

Group/Class Size: Any
Duration: 30-45 minutes

Lesson Objective(s):
*   Students will share music making with others, using basic performance skills and techniques, and respond to live or recorded music.

Learning outcomes:
*   Students will respond to and discuss contrasting music using the thinking hats.

Write your own learning outcome(s) here:

You will need:
*   Thinking hats cards or wheel
*   Contrasting music
*   A big piece of paper

Activity

★ As a class, listen to two different pieces of music from different eras, cultures, genres or styles. Make up a comparison chart of information about the differences between the two pieces of music.

★ Use the thinking hats as follows:

Red hat: What emotions or moods does the music evoke?

Blue hat: What is the context of the music? What period was it created in? When and how would the music usually be performed?

White hat: What instruments can you hear? Who are the musicians? What background information do you know about the piece?

Green hat: What is unusual or creative about this music?

Yellow hat: Do you like one song more than the other? What is good about each one?

Black hat: Is there anything you don't like about the music or the way it is played?

Colour Your World

Teacher's Notes

Group/Class Size: Any/pairs or groups
Duration: 30-45 minutes

Lesson Objective(s):

• Students will invent and represent musical ideas to express mood, using shape and contrast.

Learning outcomes:

• Students will write pieces of music using the thinking hats to create shape and contrast.

Write your own learning outcome(s) here:

You will need:

• Thinking hats cards or wheel
• Assorted musical instruments
• A large dose of creativity!

Activity

★ In pairs or in groups, choose a selection of instruments.

★ Choose two different thinking hats and brainstorm what they represent.

★ Use two different hats to make a contrast.

★ Use this information to write a piece of music.
   For example:

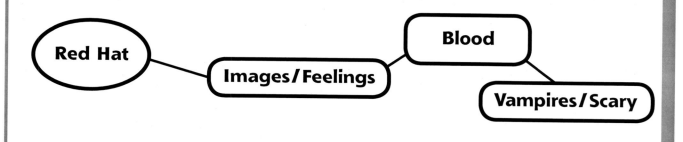

Culture Club

Subject: Music, History, Geography

Year: 3/4

Teacher's Notes

Group/Class Size: Any
Duration: 30-45 minutes

Lesson Objective(s):
• Students will identify and investigate characteristics of music associated with particular contexts, purposes, and styles in past and present cultures.

Learning outcomes:
• Students will use the thinking hats to investigate and identify characteristics of music in different cultures.

Write your own learning outcome(s) here:

Point to ponder:
• If you are studying a particular culture in another subject, you might like to link this lesson together as a cross-curriculum activity.
• You may have people in your class from a particular culture who could be your experts.

You will need:
• Thinking hats cards or wheel
• Examples of music from different cultures (recordings, videos or even live performance)
• Scrapbooks

Activity

★ As a class, listen to/view or research music from our country and/or music from another culture.

★ Using the thinking hats, make a scrapbook with pictures and charts of all of the interesting things that you can find out about music in that culture.

★ You might like to compare two different cultures, or you might like to stick to one For example:

White hat: What instruments do they use? Are there specific rituals or festivals associated with the music?

Red hat: How does the music make you feel?

Green hat: What is different or unusual about music in this culture?

Yellow hat: What do you like about this music?

Black hat: What do you dislike about this music?

Blue hat: What is music? What are the common linking factors?

Hidden Meanings

Teacher's Notes

Group/Class Size: Any
Duration: 30-45 minutes

Lesson Objective(s):

• Students will describe ways in which objects and images can communicate stories and ideas.

Learning outcomes:

• Students will use thinking hats to look at the hidden stories and ideas that pieces of art convey.

Write your own learning outcome(s) here:

You will need:

• Thinking hats cards or wheel
• Examples of art works (any form)
• A detective's outfit for the teacher (only if you are brave)

Activity

★ As a class discuss levels of meaning in art.

★ Using the thinking hats, discuss what you can see in a piece of art and what meanings or stories are hidden if you think deeply about it.

★ For example:

Red hat: Do you think that person is really happy? Why is he holding a knife behind his back? What has the artist put in this picture to make him look sad?

Blue hat: What kind of art work is this? Why do you think that the artist did it this way?

White hat: What can you see in this picture? What is he standing next to? Do you know what country this is set in?

Green hat: How would you change this painting if you could? Is there anything unusual or weird or new about this painting?

Yellow hat: Why is it good that the artist did it this way? What is good about the way that the paint is applied?

Black hat: Do you think the artist thinks this person is ugly? Why would he paint a scene about war?

Code Red!

Subject: Art

Year: 2/3

Teacher's Notes

Group/Class Size: Any
Duration: 30-45 minutes

Lesson Objective(s):

* Students will develop visual ideas in response to a variety of motivations, using imagination, observation, and invention with materials.

Learning outcomes:

* Students will use the red thinking hat as a motivation to create art works based on different emotions.

Write your own learning outcome(s) here:

Point to ponder:

* The art works could be any medium you like such as: paint, collage, sculpture or drawing.
* Help students to broaden their understanding of conveying emotion beyond just drawing a face to different aspects of the art that evoke emotion in the person who views the art.

You will need:

* Red thinking hat card
* Art materials
* A heaped helping of imagination and a dash of emotion

Activity

★ Using the red thinking hat, discuss how artists show emotions in their artworks. What colours are happy colours? What colours make you feel scared?

★ Choose three ways that artists show emotion. These could be: colour, facial expressions, objects or light and shading.

★ In the medium of your choice, create an art work that shows an emotion, using the three different ways.

★ Try and guess which emotion the art works are based on.

Green Machine

Teacher's Notes

Subject: Art
Year: 3/4

Group/Class Size: Any/in groups

Duration: 30-45 minutes

Lesson Objective(s):
- Students will generate and develop visual ideas in response to a variety of motivations, using imagination, observation, and invention with materials.

Learning outcomes:
- Students will use the green thinking hat as a motivation to invent a machine out of a variety of found materials.

Write your own learning outcome(s) here:

You will need:

- Green thinking hat
- Found materials such as: shoeboxes, cardboard, napkins, newspaper, cotton spools, old machine parts and springs
- Art materials

Activity

★ Make a class collection of found materials like those listed above.

★ In groups, choose a type of machine that you would like to invent such as a chocolate making machine or a machine for drying pickles.

★ Discuss green hat ways that you can use the materials you have to make your machine.

★ Once you have put it together, paint it, test it and show it to the rest of the class.

★ Use your best green hat, thinking: how can I be more inventive or creative with the materials I have?

Colour Collage

Teacher's Notes

Group/Class Size: Any
Duration: 30-45 minutes

Lesson Objective(s):
- Students will generate and develop visual ideas in response to a variety of motivations, using imagination, observation and invention with materials.

Learning outcomes:
- Students will use the thinking hats as a basis for developing visual ideas about colour, using collage.

Write your own learning outcome(s) here:

You will need:

- Thinking hats cards or wheel
- Thinking hats key words
- A selection of colour words and pictures, such as things that are green or shades of red, etc.
- Art materials (include magazines to cut up)
- Paper

Activity

★ Choose a colour from one of the thinking hats or spin the wheel or pick a card.

★ Make an art work that is based on that colour.

★ You could try making a collage of words, pictures and original art all related to your chosen colour including the thinking hats key words.

★ Talk about all the things that your chosen colour represents and how you could use different artistic techniques to portray it.

★ Be creative. The possibilities are endless!

Relationship Circle

Teacher's Notes

Subject: PHSE and Citizenship
Geography   **Year:** 2/3

Group/Class Size: Any
Duration: 20-30 minutes

Lesson Objective(s):

- Students will demonstrate knowledge and understandings of how and why groups are organized within communities and societies.

Learning outcomes:

- Students will use the thinking hats to discuss how groups are organized within communities and societies.
- Students will hold paper streamers across a circle to demonstrate relationships within groups.

Write your own learning outcome(s) here:

You will need:

- Thinking hats cards or wheel
- Rolled up paper streamers in the thinking hats colours
- Small scrap pieces of paper

Activity

- ★ Using the thinking hats, discuss groups, communities and societies and come up with a brainstormed list of the different relationships, such as mothers – children, fathers – children, doctor – patient, policemen – criminals and teacher – student.

- ★ Sit in a circle and put the streamers and pieces of paper and pens in the middle.

- ★ In turns, name one person such as a teacher and get someone on the other side of the circle to name someone who they relate to such as a student. Write the person on a piece of paper and put it in front of you.

- ★ Give one end of the streamer to each person such as teacher and student.

- ★ By now, one person should be holding each end of the streamer on opposite sides of the circle. Those people keep holding onto the streamer while the activity continues.

- ★ Keep going until everyone is holding onto streamers. Some people might need to hold more than one.

- ★ Use the thinking hats to discuss the relationships.
  For example:

  Black hat: I feel silly when my dad tells me (the child) off.

- ★ Think of an alternative way people could get to hold the streamers and therefore show relationships.

Thinking Hats – Book 2   **17**

It's in the Past

Teacher's Notes

Group/Class Size: Any
Duration: 20-30 minutes

Lesson Objective(s):
- Students will demonstrate knowledge and understandings of how and why the past is important to people.

Learning outcomes:
- Students will use the thinking hats to interview at least one elderly person about why the past is important to them.

Write your own learning outcome(s) here:

You will need:
- Thinking hats cards or wheel
- At least one elderly person willing to be interviewed

Activity

★ Before your guest arrives, prepare thinking hats questions that you might like to ask them.
For example:

Red hat: How did you feel when the war was going on?

Yellow hat: What positive things happened in the community where you grew up?

White hat: What was different when you were our age? What was your childhood like?

★ You might like to have one person facilitating the interview like a 'talk show host' and set up a studio or make a video of the interview.

★ Discuss what you found out from the interview about why the past is important to people.

Resource Me!

Teacher's Notes

Subject: Geography

Year: 3/4

Group/Class Size: Any/two groups
Duration: 20-30 minutes

Lesson Objective(s):
- Students will demonstrate knowledge and understandings of how and why people manage resources.

Learning outcomes:
- Students will use the thinking hats to look at how and why people manage resources, by role-playing with props and resources.

Write your own learning outcome(s) here:

You will need:
- Thinking hats cards and wheel
- A box containing resources:
  A selection of play money, cards with pictures of different resources eg. houses, pets, land, rivers, shops, buildings, electricity and gas etc. (You could use objects to represent different resources.)

Activity

- ★ Split the class into two groups.
- ★ Give one group a piece of paper each with a thinking hat at the top of the page.
- ★ Give the other group the box of resources.
- ★ For the resource group: Imagine that you are in charge of all of the resources for your city, country or community.

  Before opening the box quickly just brainstorm the different types of resources in the community to get you started.

  Open your resource box and take out a picture representing one type of resource at a time. Name the resource. Discuss how you would manage this resource or what you would do with it. Who will do what and why?

  For the thinking hats group: You are silent observers. Watch exactly what the first group does and record your observations under the corresponding thinking hat. For example: The money was all given to one person. (This might come under the black hat.)

- ★ After an allocated time, stop both groups and discuss what you discovered about resources. How does what you learned relate to the community we live in now?
- ★ Groups could swap over and play the different roles.

Play By the Rules!

Teacher's Notes

Group/Class Size: Any
Duration: 20-30 minutes

Lesson Objective(s):

• Students will demonstrate knowledge and understandings of how and why people make and implement rules and laws.

Learning outcomes:

• Students will use thinking hats to create a large class brainstorm about different rules, who made them and why they are made.

Write your own learning outcome(s) here:

You will need:

• Thinking hats cards or wheel
• Large pieces of paper
• Coloured felt pens or crayons

Activity

★ Stick large pieces of paper on one wall of the classroom.

★ Think of different rules that you know of in the classroom, community/city and may be even nationally. Write these in boxes or bubbles in the centre of the papers.

★ Using the thinking hats, discuss the rules and why they are there. What would happen if they were changed? How do they affect your life?

★ If you have a red thinking hat point, write it up with a red pen or crayon, green hat, use a green crayon etc.

★ Draw lines to create a large scale brainstorming diagram.

Colourful Conversations

Subject: English: Speaking and listening

Year: 2/3

Teacher's Notes

Group/Class Size: Any/in groups
Duration: 30-45 minutes

Lesson Objective(s):

- Students will converse, ask questions, and talk about events and personal experiences in a group.

Learning outcomes:

- Students will use the thinking hats as a starting point for talking about their personal life experiences.
- Students will use thinking hats as a starting point for asking questions of others about their life experiences.

Write your own learning outcome(s) here:

You will need:

- Thinking hats cards or wheel
- Possibly some practice at oral language
- A timer

Activity

★ Split into groups and sit in circles.

★ Each take a thinking hat card or spin the wheel to choose a colour.

★ Going clockwise, ask the person on your left a question using the thinking hat that you chose. The speaker must talk to the rest of the group for the set amount of time (one or two minutes).

★ For example:

Yellow hat: What was something really great that happened to you?

Red hat: What events do you feel really deeply about?

Blue hat: Talk about your life and how it is affected by your community.

White hat: Facts. Where were you born? Do you have any pets?

Black hat: Talk about an incident where something went wrong or didn't turn out how you wanted it to.

Green hat: What was the weirdest or most creative thing you have ever done?

★ Choose another hat or spin the wheel to get another colour. Swap places so you get to ask someone else or ask the person on your right.

★ Divide into small groups, so you get more turns at practising speaking on a certain topic for the set time.

Rainbow Diary

Subject: English: Writing

Year: 2/3

Teacher's Notes

Group/Class Size: Any
Duration: 20-30 minutes

Lesson Objective(s):
* Students will write regularly and spontaneously to record personal experiences and observations.

Learning outcomes:
* Students will use the thinking hats as a basis for recording daily observations.

Write your own learning outcome(s) here:

You will need:
* Thinking hats cards or wheel
* Notebooks or journals

Activity

* Using a notebook or journal, make up a chart with headings for each thinking hat colour (or one page each if you are a keen writer).

* Spend some time each day recording events that you have observed under each hat.

* For example:

   Green hat: There was a plant growing through the floorboards in the classroom and Annie wore odd socks to school today.

   Black hat: It rained all lunchtime and everyone had to stay inside.

   Red hat: I felt so sad because I stubbed my toe today.

   Yellow hat: My teacher gave me a sticker for my spelling words again!

   White hat: Only three people ordered lunch from the tuckshop.

   Blue hat: There is only five weeks till Christmas.

* Keep your diary for a week and then share them as a class.

Red Letter

Teacher's Notes

Group/Class Size: Any
Duration: 20-30 minutes

Lesson Objective(s):

* Students will write on a variety of topics, shaping, editing, and reworking texts in a range of genres, and using vocabulary and conventions, such as spelling and sentence structure, appropriate to the genre.

Learning outcomes:

* Students will use thinking hats to write and edit letters to imaginary people.

Write your own learning outcome(s) here:

You will need:

* Thinking hats cards or wheel
* Paper and pencils/pens

Activity

★ Pick a thinking hat card or spin the wheel.

★ Write a letter to an imaginary person using the thinking hats.

★ For example:

Green hat: Be weird, creative or outrageous. Dear Penelope, I love your apple strudel, but I am currently detained on Mars. It is with regret that I inform you I will not be home in time to eat it. From the love of your life, Barnabas.

White hat: I am in France. Temperatures have been below zero for the last three nights. We can not get out the door for the snow piled up against it. We have enough food left for only one more day.

Blue hat: As the chairman of board for this organization I am writing to let you know the board's views . . .

Red hat: To my best friend Angela. I have been just so miserable since we fought the other day and now we aren't talking. I hate having no friend to talk to. I have a hunch that if we don't fix this now we will never be friends again.

Yellow hat: Dear Mum, Camp is amazing. We were allowed to have a midnight feast our first night and even the teachers joined in. I climbed to the top of the rock wall today and had a go in a canoe on the lake.

Black hat: To Whom It May Concern, This letter is to inform you that I disliked your performance on stage last night. You got the words in your second song all wrong. I also think your dancing technique needs some improvement because you made some errors.

Hat Tag

Teacher's Notes

Group/Class Size: Any
Duration: 20-30 minutes

Lesson Objective(s):

* Students should write regularly and with ease to express personal responses to different experiences and to record observations and ideas.

Learning outcomes:

* Students will use the thinking hats to write short sentences about their experiences and get their classmates to guess what colour inspired them.

Write your own learning outcome(s) here:

You will need:

* Thinking hats cards
* Paper

Activity

* ★ Give each student a piece of paper and a thinking hat card.

* ★ No-one else is allowed to see which card you picked.

* ★ Using the thinking hat, write about an experience you have had.

* ★ Everyone should have one story and one thinking hat card (don't show anyone your card).

* ★ This is how the activity works:

* ★ Sit in a big circle.

* ★ Choose someone to start off by standing in the middle and reading their story.

* ★ If you know that his or her story is a red hat story and you have a red hat, you can jump up and tag that person. Try and get there first.

* ★ If you tag them, then it is your turn to read your story.

Let's Get Physical!

Teacher's Notes
Group/Class Size: Any
Duration: 20-30 minutes

Lesson Objective(s):
* Students will experience and describe the benefits of regular physical activity.

Learning outcomes:
* Students will keep a physical activity journal and use thinking hats to record their experiences.

Write your own learning outcome(s) here:

You will need:
* Thinking hats cards or wheel
* Journals or notebooks
* Boundless energy

Activity

* ★ Students will include some type of physical activity into their day every day for one week.
* ★ Each day write the date in your journal and what you did.
* ★ Using the thinking hats, discuss and write down what you did or what you discovered about the benefits of exercise.
* ★ For example:

  White hat: Today I ran for 10 minutes and did 100 skips.

  Red hat: I ran the whole length of the field today and I felt puffed.

  Black hat: I was so tired after playing basketball that I almost fell asleep in class.

  Green hat: I made up a new game today. . .

  Yellow hat: Susie and I did the same exercise together which was fun.

  Blue hat: I find exercise really good for me because I can run further now.

* ★ Keep your diary for a week and then write about your whole week wearing the blue hat.
* ★ Has your fitness improved? Did you learn any new skills? What did you learn about why exercise is good for you?

It's All About Me

Teacher's Notes

Group/Class Size: Any
Duration: 30 minutes

Lesson Objective(s):
*   Students will identify personal strengths that contribute to a sense of self-worth

Learning outcomes:
*   Students will use the thinking hats to make colour charts about themselves and their strengths and weaknesses.

Write your own learning outcome(s) here:

You will need:
*   Thinking hats cards or wheel
*   Coloured card and A3 paper
*   Felt pens and art materials

Activity

*   ★ Draw a self-portrait and glue it into the centre of an A3 piece of paper, leaving lots of space around the edge.

*   ★ Divide the space around your portrait into six sections, for each of the thinking hats.

*   ★ Write about yourself in the sections, using the thinking hats.

*   ★ For example:

    Yellow hat: I am really good at swimming and I won my race.

    Black hat: I am not very good at spelling sometimes.

    Green hat: I can turn my eyelids inside out and freek my teacher out.

    White hat: I have a moon-shaped scar on my left knee.

*   ★ As a class, discuss strengths and weaknesses using the thinking hats and think about why it is important to know that we all have weaknesses, but we all have strengths too.

Can You Relate?

Teacher's Notes

Subject: PHSE

Year: 3/4

Group/Class Size: Any/in groups
Duration: 30 minutes

Lesson Objective(s):
* Students will identify and compare ways of establishing relationships and managing changing relationships.

Learning outcomes:
* Students will use thinking hats to discuss different relationship scenarios and what they could do in those situations.

Write your own learning outcome(s) here:

You will need:
* Thinking hats cards or wheel
* Pieces of card/cards with different relationship scenarios (see below)

Activity

★ On cards – write a series of relationship scenarios such as starting a new school, changing classes or a friend who doesn't want to play with you.

★ As a class, use the thinking hats to come up with ideas of how to cope in different situations (or what not to do – black hat).

★ Split up into groups and take turns at picking out scenario cards or thinking hats cards and discuss the different problems as a group.

★ For example:

Red hat: Other people in your class might be feeling lonely too and you could make friends with them.

White hat: You could find out if there are any sports teams or groups that you could join to meet new people.

Blue hat: If someone doesn't want to be your friend it might be a misunderstanding.

Yellow hat: You could apologise and try and be friends again.

Black hat: It is not good to talk to other people about it behind their back

Green hat: You could make up a game and invite people to play it with you.

★ Come back together as a class and discuss what you learned.

In the Media

Teacher's Notes

Group/Class Size: Whole class, then in groups
Duration: 30 minutes

Lesson Objective(s):
* Students will identify how health care and physical activity practices are influenced by community and environmental factors.

Learning outcomes:
* Students will use the thinking hats to discuss how health care and physical activity are portrayed in the media and how this might influence people.

Write your own learning outcome(s) here:

You will need:
* Thinking hats cards or wheel
* Magazine or newspaper clippings of health, food or exercise related advertisements
* Scissors and glue

Activity

* ★ As a class, use the thinking hats to discuss advertisements about health and exercise and how they might influence people.
* ★ In groups, cut out ads and stick them onto a large piece of paper.
* ★ Write the information you discover around the ad, for example:

Red hat: Someone who is overweight might feel pressured to take this medication to help them lose weight because of the picture.

Yellow hat: This ad is good because it tells people that you need to wear sunscreen to protect yourself in the sun.

Black hat: This ad may have negative effects on some people because the model is too thin and some people may feel they need to look like her.

White hat: They included a picture of the heart tick in this ad and all the information that you need to know about products that have the heart foundation tick.

Green hat: This ad is creative because it shows how your body might look if you didn't eat enough carbohydrates.

Blue hat: The message behind this ad is that you will be healthier if you take vitamins every day.

Red Hat Graph

Teacher's Notes

Group/Class Size: Any
Duration: 30 minutes

Lesson Objective(s):
* Students should be able to use graphs to illustrate relationships.

Learning outcomes:
* Students will make graphs to illustrate the relationship between how they feel and what time of day it is.

Write your own learning outcome(s) here:

Point(s) to Ponder
* Teachers should use discretion as to how students display these or discuss these, or choose a different pair of words for the first time.

You will need:
* Red thinking hat or red thinking hat card
* Graph paper

Activity

★ Mark hourly time slots along the bottom (*x* axis) of your graph paper. Start at 8.30 am and finish at 3.00 pm.

★ Down the left hand side – the *y* axis, put happy at the top and sad at the bottom.

★ On the graph plot dots for each time slot to show how you felt at each time throughout the day.

★ Share your graphs as a class. What are the similarities or differences?

★ Try another day, but instead of sad to happy choose another continuum of emotions eg. uninterested to excited, or calm to angry, etc.

★ You could extend the hourly time slots to cover outside of school time and do your summary and comparisons the next day.

It Could Never Happen!

Subject: Mathematics: Handling Data

Year: 2/3

Teacher's Notes

Group/Class Size: Any
Duration: 30 minutes

Lesson Objective(s):
* Students should be able to compare familiar or imaginary, but related, events and order them on a scale from least likely to most likely.

Learning outcomes:
* Students will use the green thinking hat to think of different events and how likely they are to happen.

Write your own learning outcome(s) here:

You will need:
* Green thinking hat
* A long piece of paper
* Felt pens
* Squares of card (could be scrap pieces)
* Blu-tac or Sellotape

Activity

★ Think of a scenario such as a walk in the bush, a trip to the moon or a day at the beach.

★ Using the creative green hat, think of all the things that might happen (they could be really creative).

★ Write each one onto a piece of card and put double-sided tape or blu-tac onto the back of each card.

★ At one end of a long piece of paper, write "Most likely" and at the other, write "Most unlikely". (This is your continuum.)

★ Take turns at sticking the cards up where you think they might go on the continuum.

★ Try again, if time allows, with a different scenario.

Put Your Green Hat On

Teacher's Notes

Subject: Mathematics: Shape, space and measures

Year: 3/4

Group/Class Size: Any
Duration: 30 minutes

Lesson Objective(s):
* Students should be able to design and make a pattern which involves translation, reflection or rotation.

Learning outcomes:
* Students will use the green thinking hat to design a pattern that shows reflection and or rotation.

Write your own learning outcome(s) here:

You will need:
* Green thinking hat
* Graph paper

Activity

★ Using your most creative thinking, choose an object or shape and design a pattern that shows reflection and or rotation.

★ Share your designs with the class. Discuss in what ways the designs are creative. Remember creativity is an individual thing, but creative designs can still reflect the degree of creative thinking a person has put in.

★ Try using unusual or interesting shapes or objects.

★ You could try rotating or reflecting only a small part of a shape or putting it in an unexpected place.

★ Use art materials to decorate your pattern creatively.

What's the Time?

Teacher's Notes

Subject: Mathematics: Shape, space and measures

Year: 3

Group/Class Size: Any/in pairs
Duration: 30 minutes

Lesson Objective(s):

- Within a range of meaningful contexts, students should be able to read and interpret everyday statements involving time.

Learning outcomes:

- Students will use the thinking hats to write statements for each other using time.
- Students will learn how to write time in words and to show it visually on a clock.

Write your own learning outcome(s) here:

You will need:

- Thinking hats cards or wheel
- Paper and pens
- Clock outlines/diagrams

Activity

★ In pairs, use the thinking hats to write statements that include time.

★ First, spin the thinking hats wheel or pick a card.

★ Some ideas to get you started:

Green hat: make the sentence as wacky and inventive as possible, such as "He liked to eat pickled onions quarter of an hour before his eight o'clock bedtime, so he always had nightmares".

Red hat: Statements involving feelings or emotions, such as "I get so annoyed when my dad sleeps in till quarter to ten on a Saturday morning".

★ One partner should then draw the time mentioned in the statement on a clock.

★ Swap roles, so that each person has a turn at writing and drawing.

Colourful Construction

Teacher's Notes

Group/Class Size: Any
Duration: 30 minutes

Lesson Objective(s):

* Students should identify views about a specific technological development within the local community.

Learning outcomes:

* Students will use thinking hats to identify different views about construction technology used in a local building project.

Write your own learning outcome(s) here:

You will need:

* Thinking hats cards or wheel
* A current building project in the local community
* Information relating to various technology used on the project
* A clear file folder or ring-binder (or way to present the information)

Activity

★ This activity is a research project to find out different viewpoints about the technology used on a building project.

★ Compile information that you find in a folder.

★ Use the thinking hats to discuss different aspects of the technology and talk to people who use it. For example:

White hat: Who can operate the technology and how easy is it to use? What does it do?

Blue hat: What is the building project? What other technology is needed?

Yellow hat: What is helpful about this technology?

Green hat: Are there any other uses for the technology?

★ Write about what you find out and put it in your research folder.

★ Make a class presentation of all your findings.

Technology and the Media

Teacher's Notes

Group/Class Size: Any
Duration: 30 minutes

Lesson Objective(s):
- Students should identify and discuss ways in which a specific technology is communicated and promoted.

Learning outcomes:
- Students will use thinking hats to discuss ways in which technologies are communicated and promoted in the media.

Write your own learning outcome(s) here:

You will need:
- Thinking hats cards or wheel
- Advertising material or articles relating to your chosen technologies

Activity

★ Choose an item of technology such as the Internet, software or a household appliance that you can find in the media.

★ Collect advertising material or articles about your chosen technology.

★ Use the thinking hats to discuss how effectively this technology is promoted.
For Example:

White hat: What pictures or words were used to describe the item?

Green hat: What is unusual or creative about the article or ad?

Blue hat: What impression did you get from the media?

At the Gym

Teacher's Notes

Subject: Design and Technology

Year: 3/4

Group/Class Size: Any
Duration: 30 minutes

Lesson Objective(s):
• Students should investigate and describe the use and operation of technologies in an everyday setting.

Learning outcomes:
• Students will use thinking hats to describe the use and operation of technology in a gym.

Write your own learning outcome(s) here:

You will need:
• Thinking hats cards and wheel
• Access to a gym with equipment
• A4 paper

Activity

★ Students will visit a local gym.

★ Divide a piece of paper into six squares (one for each thinking hat).

★ Choose one piece of technology in the gym and ask an expert or a teacher about what it does.

★ Write down information in any of the thinking hats squares, such as:

White hat: This is called a bench press.

Yellow hat: This machine is good because it helps you to build your leg muscles and make them stronger.

Black hat: This machine is really hard to use by yourself.

Green hat: Can you think of an improvement to a piece of equipment? What other uses can you think of?

Pollution!

Subject: Design and Technology

Year: 3/4

Teacher's Notes

Group/Class Size: Any
Duration: 30 minutes

Lesson Objective(s):

- Students should describe and identify the positive and negative effects of some instances of technologies on people's lives and environment.

Learning outcomes:

- Students will use thinking hats to discuss the positive and negative effects of technologies that cause pollution.

Write your own learning outcome(s) here:

You will need:

- Thinking hats cards or wheel
- Information about pollution and technologies that cause pollution

Activity

★ Research and discuss technologies that cause pollution.

★ Use the thinking hats to discuss the effects that these technologies have on people:

Red hat: Sometimes people can feel sick if they breathe in too many car fumes.

Yellow hat: If you stay inside the car and not on a bike then you won't breathe in as much pollution.

Black hat: If we use too many spraycans, we can affect the ozone layer.

Green hat: What could we do to reduce pollution?

★ Make a chart or display to show what you learned.

What's Cooking?

Teacher's Notes

Group/Class Size: Any
Duration: 30 minutes

Lesson Objective(s):

* Students can use simple technology to demonstrate and explain methods which prevent or promote change in materials.

Learning outcomes:

* Students will use the white hat to document information and explain methods which promote or prevent change in materials during simple cooking such as making toast.

Write your own learning outcome(s) here:

Point to Ponder:

* There may be fire hazards involved with cooking, so make sure that the area you will be working in is hazard free.

You will need:

* White thinking hat
* Access to a cooking room or cooking facilities
* Baking or cooking ingredients

Activity

★ Choose a simple baking or cooking recipe such as cheese on toast or a simple cake.

★ Using your white hat, as you do your cooking write down all the information on the changes in the materials/ingredients.

★ For example, the bread was soft and white before we put it in the toaster. We turned it up to level 4 and it was still soft in the middle.

★ Choose different groups to experiment with different parts of the recipe and discuss what happens eg. you could leave the bread in for longer or turn up the temperature.

★ Discuss changes in the materials and explain how the technology was used to create these changes or prevent them from occurring.

★ You might like to record the changes over a period of time such as every 30 seconds.

★ This activity is all about being factual, observant and gathering information (White hat).

Changing Environments

Subject: Science: Life processes and living things

Teacher's Notes

Year: 2/3

Group/Class Size: Any
Duration: 30 minutes (over a number of lessons)

Lesson Objective(s):

* Students can investigate the responses of plants or animals, including people, to environmental changes in their habitats.

Learning outcomes:

* Students will use the thinking hats to discuss the environmental changes associated with global warming and the effect it has on animals and people.

Write your own learning outcome(s) here:

Point to ponder:

* This would link in well with a study on Antarctica.

You will need:

* Thinking hats cards or wheel
* Information about global warming and its effects

Activity

★ As a class, do some research into the environmental changes that occur with global warming and how human and animal habitats change.

★ Use the thinking hats to discuss how those changes affect humans and animals. For example:

Red hat: People might feel sad if they can't go outside without getting burnt.

Yellow hat: What positive steps have been taken or can we take to prevent global warming? Are there any good effects on habitats?

Black hat: Which habitats would be affected the worst?

Green hat: Can you think of a solution?

White hat: What is global warming? Who does it affect?

Scientific Discoveries

Subject: Science: Scientific enquiry

Year: 3/4

Teacher's Notes

Group/Class Size: Any
Duration: 30 minutes

Lesson Objective(s):

* Students can investigate the impact of some well-known technological innovation or scientific discovery on people and/or the local environment.

Learning outcomes:

* Students will use the thinking hats to discuss the impact of a scientific discovery on people and the local environment.

Write your own learning outcome(s) here:

You will need:

* Thinking hats cards or wheel
* Information about a specific scientific discovery

Activity

★ As a class, research and inquire about a specific scientific discovery such as the discovery that the earth is round.

★ Use the thinking hats to discuss the impact of this discovery on people and the local environment.
For example:

Blue hat: How is your life affected by scientific discovery? How would the world be different without it?

Red hat: How would you feel before medicine was discovered?

Black hat: What are the potential bad things about this discovery? Is there anything to watch out for?

Green hat: What would you like to discover?

★ Display your findings on a large piece of paper.

Reuse and Recycle!

Subject: Science: Life processes and living things

Year: 3/4

Teacher's Notes

Group/Class Size: Any
Duration: 30 minutes (plus ongoing project)

Lesson Objective(s):

* Students can justify their personal involvement in a school or class-initiated local environment project.

Learning outcomes:

* Students will use the thinking hats to discuss local recycling initiatives and what they could do to help.

Write your own learning outcome(s) here:

You will need:

* Thinking hats cards or wheel
* Information about local recycling projects

Activity

★ Research recycling in the local area.

★ Use the thinking hats to discuss the projects or initiatives.

★ Present your findings. (This presentation could be made in several ways.)
For example:

    – make a video, display, chart, or drama.

    – present your information using a slideshow or Powerpoint display.

★ Come up with some ideas that you could put into action yourself. Use the thinking hats to explore these ideas fully before taking any steps to reach your goal.

Colour Wheel

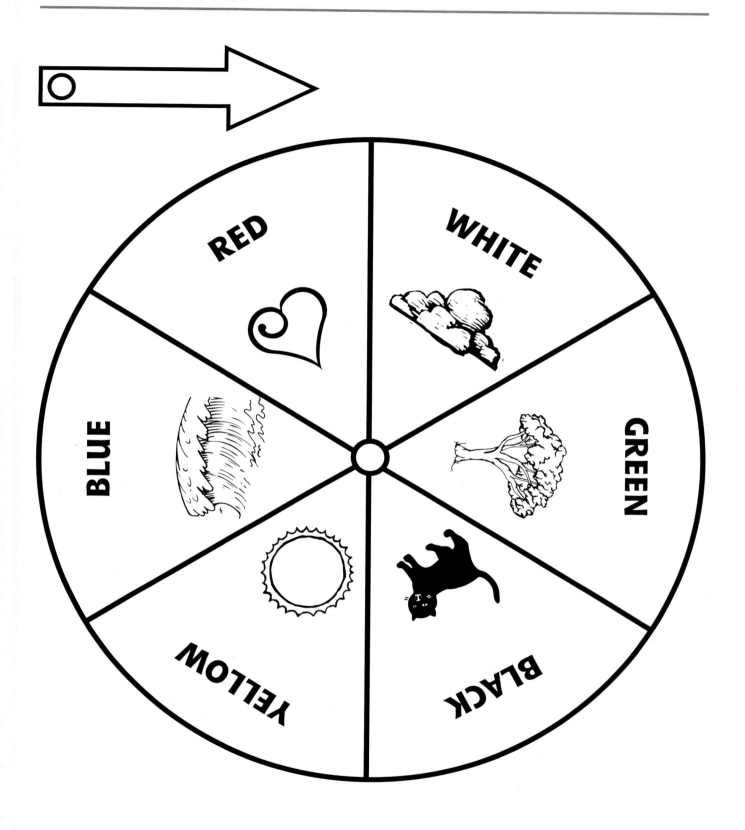

★ Colour each segment in the correct colour for each thinking hat.

★ Paste onto cardboard and cut out the two pieces.

★ Use a short pencil or stick with a point to make the wheel spinnable.

RED

Thinking Hat Cards

BLACK

Thinking Hat Cards

WHITE

Thinking Hat Cards

YELLOW

Thinking Hat Cards

GREEN

Thinking Hat Cards

BLUE

Thinking Hat Cards

Black

- What are the negative points?
- What could go wrong?
- Who might think this is a negative idea? Why?
- What don't you like about this?
- What needs to be changed or fixed?
- Who would be negatively affected?

Thinking Hat Cards

Red

- How would you feel if that was you?
- How do you think that person feels?
- What emotion can you see or hear?
- What effect would this have on the people?
- How would I feel about this in 10 years time? In 5 years?
- How would people in the past feel about this?

Thinking Hat Cards

Yellow

- What are the positive points?
- Who would agree with this? Why?
- What do we really like about this?
- What are the best parts?
- What are the benefits?
- Who would benefit?

Thinking Hat Cards

White

- What are the facts?
- How does this work?
- What do we know already about this?
- Who might know more information about this topic?
- What is it?
- What does it do?
- What is it made of?

Thinking Hat Cards

Blue

- What is the main point of this?
- What does this mean?
- Why do we need to know this?
- Why does it matter?
- Who cares?
- How does this relate to what we know about . . .?

Thinking Hat Cards

Green

- How could we do this differently?
- How could we look at this differently?
- What new ideas can you come up with?
- Can you think of a new solution?
- What if . . .?
- What might happen next?
- Where could this lead to?
- What are some other perspectives or thoughts?

Thinking Hat Cards

Thinking Hats Reference Chart

GREEN

This is such a fun hat. Think of the possibilities. Explore new heights. Question everything, turn it inside out and upside down and ask, what if? Take what you have and turn it into something new. Turn a corner or change direction. Subvert a well known idea or story. The possibilities with using the green hat are truly endless. When you have your green hat on, forget about what your mother would feel about it, forget about the facts, just jump right out of the box and see what happens. The green hat is for exploring new territory, creating and asking where to from here? Some useful visuals: A little green seedling, a tree or an expansive green field.

WHITE

When we put our white hat on, we seek out facts and information. What do we know about this already? The five senses come into play when using this hat. What can we smell/taste/hear/see? Switch your emotions off and focus on the data. Put your scientist's lab coat on (which is usually white by the way). Look at what you can observe and the evidence in front of you. Don't make a judgment on anything yet. Just gather, calculate and measure. Some helpful visuals: A white lab coat, a blank canvas or a fresh white piece of paper.

RED

The Red hat is based on feelings and emotions. Discuss how each person would feel and why. Put facts out of the picture and look at the effect on a person emotionally, spiritually or socially. Delve deeper and ask questions about values and beliefs and how situations affect people differently, depending on their upbringing, personal characteristics or circumstances. Some helpful visuals are: Hearts (linked to love, romance and affection and also anger and danger) or a red flag, seeing red.

BLUE

Take all the things you have learned from using the other 5 hats, and gather them up in a big, blue bag. This is what the blue hat is all about. What are the ties that bind everything together? Sum up your argument or your findings. Look at the bigger picture. How does this relate to us in the country we live in or even to the human race? What themes can we make out of all of this? Why do we even need to know this? Why are you in a philosophical mood, the blue hat may be just what you need. Some helpful visuals: A blue sky (arches over everything), a wave.

YELLOW

This hat looks at the world through rose-tinted glasses. What sets you alight or lights you up? Take a look at the funny, sunny side with this hat, and forget your cares. Be an optimist for a day and explore what you enjoy and what makes the world a better place. Why do some people like things that others can't stand? Ask yourself why you like what you do and why it has such a positive effect on you. Useful visuals: Sunshine, sunflowers, a smiley face. Key words are: Excellent! Positive! Fantastic!

BLACK

The black hat is essentially a pessimist's hat. This will never work! Sometimes we need a dose of reality before we plough ahead. When we have the black hat on we look at what could go wrong and who may be affected negatively. What do we dislike about this? What needs improvement or just that extra something? Feel free to be the judge when you wear this hat, just be careful you don't hurt anybody's feelings! Why do some people dislike things that others just love? Explore the realms of the negative, the ugly and the downright horrible. Find out the often unrevealed details and put them on display. Some helpful pictures: A judge in a black robe, the grim reaper, a witch's hat.

Hat Template

Thinking Hats - Key Words

argument	what	facts	opinion	happy	assess
who	information	view	when	thinking	decision
feeling	evidence	debate	sad	messages	why

Thinking Hats - Key Words

positive	knowledge	emotion	empathy	alternative	ideas
values	where	negative	research	effect	judge
discovery	consequence	understand	solution	creativity	data